CLIMBING AND TAO

2021 Juan Marbarro ©
Edition: Fabio Jiménez
Translation: Carmen Lozano
Cover design: Gloria Jiménez

Climbing Letters
climbingletters.com

ISBN: 978-84-123960-2-7
All rights reserved ©

CLIMBING AND TAO
THE WAY OF THE ROUTE

Juan Marbarro

Contents

Introduction 7
What is the Tao? 13
Observe 17
Yin & Yang 21
Balance 25
Too much Yang 31
Subtlety 37
Letting go of (excessive) control 43
The Void 49
Wu Wei 59
Harmony 69
Flow 81
Glossary 89
Taoist Readings 95

Introduction

This book is a continuation of my intention to conceive Climbing as a means of personal exploration that goes far beyond the exploration of mountains, climbing routes or the physical world in general.

Some may find it absurd and just conceive climbing as ascending walls, using physical strength to climb upwards, a way of getting a workout. I'm not saying that it can't be enjoyed that way, but I'm sure that its potential is much greater.

Nor do I mean to say that my way of understanding climbing is the best or most useful for everyone. However, I try to observe life through climbing, to see it as a whole that I can also use as a laboratory where I can experiment with myself and my experience, my perception, extracting useful lessons for everyday life. For me, climbing is a way of gaining awareness and growing personally. It is a means of observation of nature, life, the world, the universe. One of my favorite prisms through which to view reality.

We all use different "lenses" to experience life and observe our universe. The scientist may use a microscope or a telescope, depending on their discipline.

The writer uses writing, the musician uses music, the investor uses numbers, and the trader uses money. The climber, climbing.

"If all you have is a hammer, everything looks like a nail." If you have a hammer, it will look like every problem will need to get hammered down to be fixed. This is what is known as "the golden hammer," also known as "law of the instrument" or "Maslow's hammer." It is the conception that any tool or paradigm is the solution to all problems, even those for which it is not so well suited. A loose nail, hammer blow. The chair leg comes loose, hammer blow. Printer doesn't work, well, hit it, to be a little more subtle. We all fall into some sort of paradigm through which we experience life. I simply believe that, in order to grow, the only thing necessary is to broaden that paradigm, even a little bit, thus expanding the range of possibilities, using whatever can offer the best result at any given moment. If we live in the paradigm of the hammer, we can also try to expand to the paradigm of the screwdriver, which will give us a broader vision and at the same time open up a lot of new possibilities.

According to the law of the instrument, the climber will only see climbable walls, holes to hold on to and places to abseil down from. And let's admit it, it's a bit like that. But there is so much more. We can open our minds and develop all the possibilities that climbing offers, both as an activity and as a paradigm or lens through which to gain awareness.

Climbing brings together many of the characteristics that are replicated in our daily lives: the difficulty, the satisfaction, the decisions; the relationship with oneself, with the environment and with others; communication or emotional management. I began to analyze many of these experiences in the previous book "Stoic Climbing", relating them to an ancient wisdom that is being found very useful in current times: stoicism. A Western philosophy that, as I studied it, was awakening my interest to see how much it could be used in daily life and climbing. Since daily life is very complex and everyone has their own, which is very different from that of others, I thought it was a good idea to analyze these tools through climbing. Besides, the Stoics have been discussing how to apply them to life for two thousand three hundred years. I thought something a little different could be done.

Now, to continue to expand my view on life, climbing and Stoicism, I would like to further expand my "tool/paradigm" —and yours, hopefully— by exploring Taoism through climbing. A more Eastern worldview (abstract, complex and culturally different) that we may not be used to, which confronts us with a bit more challenging work, perhaps, than understanding Stoicism, always more pragmatic and blunt. But hey, we climbers like challenges, we deal well with discomfort. I think it will be interesting and we will have a good time.

For thousands of years, various martial arts have been based on Taoist precepts. It is what human beings have done for as long as they have been conscious: use the tools at their disposal to fight or defend themselves. So, it makes sense that they have applied all available wisdom to wars or how best to fight. But now that, fortunately, many of us don't have to go around fighting and warring, perhaps we can find better applications for such valuable wisdom. Here is my proposal: Taoist Climbing.

Again, I think it is necessary to clarify that in these pages you will not find a method, a training or a recipe for better climbing. And in this case, unlike the first book, not even to live better. You will only find some ideas and concepts that can lead you to those results depending on how you apply them. Climbing will only be a means through which these ideas are interpreted so that they can be presented to us in a clear and somewhat easier to understand way, the latter task not entirely simple since we are dealing with philosophical concepts that are already complicated in themselves, without dogmatism or pretensions.

Nor is it my intention to explain Taoism in detail. Here you will find a personal interpretation of some basic concepts exposed in Taoism, analyzed through the prism of climbing as a playground, with no intention of creating any kind of method or technique, not even contemplating any kind of academic rigor.

The Tao is broad and deep enough for this interpretation to be both legitimate and incomplete, since it is an ineffable mystery and the texts that attempt to describe it are ambiguous, change even in different translations and are subject to endless interpretations, as it cannot be otherwise.

I will add several passages throughout the text so that you can see for yourself the ambiguity and depth of which I speak, as well as allowing you to draw your own conclusion.

Taoism is a philosophy that, having as its basis the concept of the Tao, has been developing over thousands of years, bifurcating or merging, giving rise to various schools of thought. That is why explaining precisely the elements of Tao and Taoism is an impossible task, not only because of its vastness, but also because of its very nature, as we will see below.

What is the Tao?

I don't know, and I can't explain it. I know what you are thinking: "why are you writing a book about the Tao then? And how are you going to relate it to climbing?" Nobody knows what it is, nobody can explain it. Such is the essence of Tao, to go beyond our understanding. It is the mystery of the universe. It cannot be known through the intellect. It is a mystery that I like to feel through climbing, among other things. The book Tao Te Ching, a fundamental pillar of Taoism, begins its first chapter like this:

> "The Tao that can be described
> is not the eternal Tao.
> The name that can be spoken
> is not the eternal Name."
>
> Lao Tzu. Tao Te Ching, 1[1]

The Tao Te King is a book believed to have been written in China around the 6th century B.C. by Lao

---

[1] All Lao Tzu quotes are from the Tao Te Ching. Translation for the public domain by J. H, McDonald (see bibliography).

Tzu[2], although there are still doubts as to whether or not this person existed.

The word Tao has been commonly translated as "the way" or "the path", alluding to the natural order of the universe, the framework in which all things unfold. It refers to the How rather than the What: the law, the operating system, the playing field, the framework. The all-encompassing unity, the essence in which everything you can imagine —and what you can't— unfolds. Remember that none of the things I mentioned in the last few sentences even come close to defining the tao, but there is no other way to introduce the idea. The tao is everything. Literally, the everything.

道

Although we tend to define and label things as separate entities, the reality is that everything is

---
[2] Also written as Lao Tse or Laozi, his name comes to mean "Old Master".

connected and can only exist because of that connection. The tree is not a tree, it is the connection and continuous collaboration between the earth, the water, the sun and many other factors, although we see it as a tree, as something individual and separate according to the information that our senses give us. Even more separate are the flowers and the bees, and they could not exist without each other. The things that we conceive as different things only exist as a whole. Thus, the mind influences the body and vice versa, ecosystems have an equilibrium that can be broken or modified, our actions have consequences and climbing can be related to life and to the tao. In the same way, changing one small thing in our life, such as an attitude, an action or a habit can affect the whole of our life experience. This is my approach to climbing: explore the natural order of things and gain awareness by climbing.

But the more I try to explain the tao the more difficult it will be for you to really understand it. Because the tao cannot be expressed in any way with our limited language, just as we cannot define such great things as love, contentment or fulfillment. Here goes a challenge for you. After doing a route that has been very satisfying, try to explain that feeling to the people around you. It's like trying to photograph the moon with your phone camera. The moon shines breathtakingly beautiful to your own eyes, but if you try to take a picture of it to send it to someone else, you'll end up pretty disappointed.

The concept is subject to multiple interpretations and ways of studying it given its complexity and ambiguity, as Taoists have been doing for thousands of years. You will not find in this book —or in any other— the perfect recipe to understand or know the tao. You will only find some clues to find it for yourself, or to know how to look for it. The concepts you will find in this book, as well as the climbing, are some of the tools that can help you on your way. But the tools are yours to use, and the path is yours to walk.

The tao is something you have to feel, to observe, to know firsthand. You have to be open to the experience. But the more we try to define it, the more biased we will be and the more difficult it will be to really find it. Contemplate life with attention, but keeping an open mind, without prejudice, without expectations. Search without searching. Simply to find. The well-known doing without doing, which I will talk about later.

Observe

The tao is in everything and can be observed through everything. From the largest to the smallest, from the macro to the micro. It is the natural order of things and is the same for everything. Nothing and no one escapes the tao. It encompasses all that you can see and all that you cannot see. The old and the new. It is universal, from the sun, the moon or water, to the smallest lizard, to climbing, which is the topic at hand.

If we learn the art of contemplation, of observing attentively, of reflecting on our experience, we can gain valuable wisdom about the world around us and about ourselves. It is about decoding the natural order (the tao) through our capacity for attention, observation and reflection, just as the ability to visualize and read a route helps us climb in a fluid way, wasting as little as possible our energy in the search for the right path.

Knowing how things work will give us a solid and lasting peace of mind. It can free us from the stress and anxiety so common today. Just as knowing a particular climbing route helps us to climb it with ease, to enjoy it without reservation because we know its order and rhythm. We know where to place our next foot, we know which hold we can throw ourselves at and which one we have to grab gently. We know that after the hard step comes a natural rest where we can take a break. On the contrary, when we do a route for the first time, we may not find the steps easily and we may exhaust ourselves halfway through the route trying a combination of movements that are not the right ones.

That is how practical it is to know the natural order of things. The tao. Understanding this natural order will help us not to make unnecessary or counterproductive efforts. Not being attentive, not observing, would be like standing in line all morning at the wrong window. It is like trying the crux of the route over and over again in the wrong way. Like going off the line that was thought for the route or climbing leaving the bolts on the left side when it actually goes on the right. No matter how much effort we put or how hard we work, if we do not respect the nature of the route we will not achieve anything, because we will be misdirecting our efforts, we will be climbing "out of the tao".

As I mentioned earlier, through the observation of nature we can decode part of the mystery. And it doesn't matter what we observe: everything is part of everything and works under the same system, even if they look like very different things. A lizard, climbers' spirit animal, can teach us something about climbing if we know how to observe. The wiggling of its body in synchrony with the movement of its legs gives it the balance it needs to move vertically as it pleases. Or the way it adapts its body position to the shape of the rock it is climbing, always keeping its center of gravity close to the wall.

Taoists loved to observe water. "Be water my friend", summarized Bruce Lee in an interview and was massively popularized thanks to a TV commercial. They understand water as the highest expression of tao. Water flows and adapts to any circumstance. It is soft and yet it can erode the hardest materials. Taking water as an example —as a teacher rather— is a recurring theme in Taoist writings as it will be throughout this book. The nature of the universe is change, so adaptability is a highly valued quality. Water fulfills this ideal, taking the form of its container, adapting to the shape of a cup or the flow of a river.

By contemplating nature we can easily observe its rhythms, its natural cycles, the causes and effects, the balance and interconnection of all things. It is useless to complain that it is cold in winter or hot in summer, nature is like that and is in balance. The temperature is regulated throughout the year and both winter and summer are connected. Thanks to them the trees have the period of growth, flowering and ripening of their fruits.

In climbing we can know when to push forward and when to rest, when to lock an arm to move a foot or when to stretch to reach a hold far away. If I release one hand, I will put more pressure on the other and if I stretch too much my feet will lose grip. Observing complementary opposites is one of the best ways to understand the tao and its balance. The foot and the hand, the left and the right, resting and doing, cold and heat. Yin and yang. You may already be familiar with the famous black and white circle, let's learn what it is all about.

Yin & Yang

Yin and Yang manifests through all things. Everything (tao) can be interpreted using this duality. They are the set of opposing but complementary forces that make up the complex web of connections that shape our reality.

We tend to look at things as independent, isolated from their opposites or from the rest of the system they are part of. But the tao is everything; everything is part of the same unity, even what we are used to think of as independent. Just as in climbing the left hand supports the weight for the right hand to move forward, and vice versa. Just as the feet serve as support when throwing the hands that will later pull to be able to lift the feet. In this way balance is formed, distributing the force from the left side to the right and from top to bottom or the other way around.

Likewise, yin and yang are the way to define the forces that provide balance to the universe. They give it rhythm, they are a dance between one and the other, like hand-foot, day-night, winter-summer. A constant flow that produces all the changes we are used to —and those we are not used to— in its continuous back-and-forth between opposing forces that compensate and complement each other. The examples of these forces are infinite: there are as many as things you can think of, as many as everything that exists and what does not exist. Yin would be passivity, the moon, cold, acceptance, femininity, softness, flexibility, night, subtlety, depth, intuition. In the same order, Yang would be on the opposite side with action, sun, heat, advancement, masculine, hardness, rigidity, day, dense, surface, reason.

These examples maybe seem a bit abstract. Let's take a look at how they would apply to climbing.

When we are climbing a route, we alternate moments of moving fast on hard sections and moments of resting or slowing down. This balance between vigorous action and rest is the same balance of yang and yin. Moreover, one force emanates from the other; they are opposing forces, but one cannot exist without the other, constantly creating and recreating each other. Climbing vigorously exhausts us, creating the need to rest on a ledge or in some comfortable grip. When we believe we have rested sufficiently we feel the need to move forward, otherwise we would begin to feel tired of resting, to feel the yang within the yin. For all things, whether yin or yang, are themselves composed of yin and yang in their own measure. Just as climbing could be considered a yang activity in general, within it we can find a multitude of yin aspects such as the need to learn and not just to execute; flexibility or technique versus strength in certain routes; intuition versus reason in certain moments, etc. These are just some examples, but I'm sure you can come up with many more.

Balance

All yin and yang aspects are interdependent and are in continuous balance —or in the process of balancing out—. Climbing a new route is a process of balancing between visualizing the steps and executing them. Thinking about how it could be done and trying it, searching and finding the grips and sequences, moving the hands and moving the feet, moving the body to the left and moving it to the right. If we only focus on trying over and over again, we may create an imbalance that will cause us to become injured, bored or frustrated, forcing us to rest or even quit the project to compensate for this imbalance. Great imbalances will cause great adjustments. If you put your feet up too high you will find it hard to move your hands. If you stretch your arms too much you will lose support in your feet. This is why it is important to observe and contemplate how these forces act through us, so we are able to manage the balance of our life without causing major imbalances —or, if they happen, to know why they happened and how to compensate for them—.

> "The Tao of Heaven works in the world
> like the drawing of a bow.
> The top is bent downward;
> the bottom is bent up.
> The excess is taken from,
> and the deficient is given to.
> The Tao works to use the excess,
> and gives to that which is depleted.
> The way of people is to take from the depleted,
> and give to those who already have an excess."
>
> Lao Tzu. Tao Te Ching, 77

Yin and yang and their balance permeate through everything. They are always present, even if we do not realize it or do not want to be aware of it. Even if we focus on different aspects, whether they are on one side or the other, they will be balanced in one way or another. One part cannot be altered without altering the whole system. Every small change generates big differences. Big changes generate many small differences. Yang always brings yin and yin always brings yang; there is no alternative, they are inseparable, part of the same whole. They are not two different things, they are the same thing. If we make yang efforts, we will have to compensate them with yin. Or if yin predominates, yang will manifest itself at some point. That's simply how it is, there is no way around it.

If you put a lot of effort into climbing (yang), training your physique and your psyche on complicated routes, you will certainly need a lot of rest.

Taking care of your muscles and relaxing your mind will be a yin obligation that you will have to respect cyclically if you want a sustainable practice, that is to say, in balance. If, on the other hand, your climbing practice is more yin, let's say just want to have fun and don't really push to your limits, you may have to use a lot of yang to overcome some steps, because, even if they are not very difficult, they will be difficult due to lack of habit. One thing arises from the other. Yin from yang and yang from yin. Easiness arises from overcoming difficulty. Difficulty arises in contrast to what is easy. A route will seem easy depending on the difficulty you can handle. And the other way around, something will seem difficult when we have a habit of tackling easier things.

> "When people see things as beautiful,
> ugliness is created.
> When people see things as good,
> evil is created.
> Being and non-being produce each other.
> Difficult and easy complement each other.
> Long and short define each other.
> High and low oppose each other.
> Fore and aft follow each other.
> Therefore the Master
> can act without doing anything
> and teach without saying a word."
>
> Lao Tzu. Tao Te Ching, 2

Although I am trying to simplify this concept of

balance, in reality it is much more complex. The point of balance is fluid, it is not always in the same place, as there are many more variables involved than we are taking into account in the examples. That is, climbing harder (yang) or less, is not only a balance between physical/mental effort and rest. Let's say that this balance between effort and rest in climbing is in turn in balance with the rest of the variables involved in life. If you have a stressful or physically demanding job, it is normal that you prefer to climb recreationally on weekends, enjoying every move and the environment in general. On the other hand, if you don't get stressed at work or with your family (let's say you handle it in a yin way), you will retain your strength to apply it to climbing, to push harder on the difficult steps or to better manage difficult emotions such as fear. Because You, like Everything, are a whole, an ecosystem within yourself. Climbing or any other area of you and your world are not separate parts of your life, but are part of you and influence each other, even if you don't realize it. If dealing with difficulty in climbing gives you mental strength, other areas of your life will be easier for you to manage. If you are stressed in your life, you will subconsciously need to go more to the mountain or to nature in general. What I said a few lines above: if you change one small thing, it will alter the whole ecosystem, and this will generate imbalances that will tend to find a new point of balance between all the variables.

In this dance of balance, the only thing we can do is to be attentive to what kind of imbalances we can generate and to what extent. Like the drunk who is having a great time now but will then suffer the worst hangover of his life, when we are immersed in a great imbalance, we may not realize it, but that does not exempt us from adjustment, from returning to balance by compensating for the imbalance. Going up too high will make us have to go down a lot. Too much of something will generate a loss later. The ideal is either to be prepared to handle the part and the counterpart, or to try not to generate large imbalances, to be moderate.

Back to our hands and feet in climbing. If I grab a really good hold but it is too far from the center of the route, all the effort that I am not saving in grabbing a slightly more difficult but centered hold will have to be spent on finding my way back to the center of the route where I'm supposed to be and where the bolts are. For this reason, the Taoists liked moderation and simplicity.

> "There is nothing better than moderation
> for teaching people or serving Heaven.
> Those who use moderation
> are already on the path to the Tao.
> Those who follow the Tao early
> will have an abundance of virtue.
> When there is an abundance of virtue,
> there is nothing that cannot be done.
> Where there is limitless ability,

then the kingdom is withing your grasp."

Lao Tzu. Tao Te Ching, 59

We currently live immersed in great imbalances, instability and constant great adjustments. It is the system in which we develop, it is practically our way of life, continuously generating great imbalances that later will have to be compensated, although we are not fully aware of it. In this society that pushes us to produce (yang), individuals must continually compensate the imbalance generated with the opposite force: to consume. The more they produce, the more they need to consume. Consuming products, consuming comfort, consuming information on social networks, consuming relationships or any other possible form of consumption. The pressure and stress caused by constantly working and producing has to be compensated in some way. Thus, someone who works all day long, who is kept in some kind of productive tension, even physical, can become overweight by compensating their anxiety with food, drink or large marathons of couch and television. Knowing how to keep this delicate balance is key to our peace of mind —we can also call it inner balance—. The problem is often that our society, our culture and the values that have been instilled in us put the focus on and overvalue the yang aspects. They create great imbalances that are compensated with great adjustments, making us think that we live in an unstable and agitated reality.

Too much Yang

If we analyze the values that govern our current society, we will observe that they are predominantly yang. The way we act, how we judge reality and even how we measure our happiness, among many other things.

Speed, quantity, production, action, rigidity, are some of the yang aspects that characterize today's society. We want to have more, live more experiences, do and produce more. More, more and more. Rarely less, rarely better. How do we measure a successful climber? By the grades can they climb, by how many sends they have, how many ascents, how fast they climbed whatever mountain, or even how many followers they have on social media.

The yin part, being very important and, moreover, the basis of yang, is less valued. It is perhaps less popular, less visible. More subtle, it would be accurate to say. Doing things slowly and consciously, quality, flexibility, technique, adapting, resting, accepting other opinions and points of view. All this is perceived as weak, as an almost unnecessary complement to life or to climbing a wall.

We suffer from chronic yang. We need to

compensate our yang with yin but still we let the yang impregnate our yin part until we burst. We spend the whole year producing, competing, doing non-stop, executing projects. When it's finally time for vacation, the moment to rest, to relax, to unwind from everything, boom! we have to go climb mountains. And, if possible, the farther the better. And I say "you have to go" because we see it as the obligation to do, the obligation to enjoy. More stress, more yang. I'm going to climb whatever peak or I don't know how many routes, I'm going to visit such and such a city and then such and such another, I'm going to do this via ferrata and then eat at that famous restaurant. Do, do, do. The GPS takes us from one place to another in a precise way so that we can collect the moments in our cell phone and in our social network profile. It's no wonder that yin has enough of us and puts its feet down to make us stop. That stomachache that slows down the pace of the trip forcing me to rest or that tiredness that makes me sleep twelve hours after dragging myself through the plans I had, which I didn't even enjoy because of how exhausted I was. Even that rain that truncates the hectic plans and forces to reorganize more calmly.

These imbalances are part of our way of life and most of the time we fail to see them. Continuing with our vacation example, why do people go on vacation farther and farther away to more and more expensive —and overcrowded— places when they don't really know many of the beautiful places around them? If you spend all year working, making sacrifices and saving, it's normal that to compensate for that you need to do something big —or that seems big—. However, if you were more in balance in your day-to-day life, without so much yang (effort, speed, productivity), you wouldn't need to spend thousands of euros on a vacation to "free yourself" from stress. You could enjoy more the little things, what is close by, simplicity in general.

In macro terms we talk about a year —although we could talk about a lifetime—, but in micro terms we can say that we suffer from the same thing in our daily lives. The same situations on a different scale: we spend more than half of our day producing, doing, pursuing goals. When it's time to recover, eating, for example, we go around repressing ourselves with absurd diets and counting calories. Then we have some time to go for a walk and instead we force ourselves to walk X kilometers. Or we go to the climbing gym and we want to do as many routes as possible, if possible more than our partners, even if we don't enjoy any of them. Or it's climbing day and we go to the mountain and our expectations are to climb routes with high grades or many routes, making us look more like "route collectors" instead of climbers who experiment, discover and enjoy.

With these yang pressures we put on ourselves in our day-to-day lives, it's normal that yin has to push through any way it can. And it may be by stuffing ourselves with food at some point, consuming alcohol or other drugs, or binge watching a series for six hours straight. That's if we don't cause ourselves some injury or illness that makes us slow down or even stop. Advertising sells us vitamins and various supplements to "not be tired", or creams to repair the skin faster, making money from our vain attempt to suppress our yin part, which needs to rest, not only sleeping, but disconnecting from the routines that in some cases do not do us any good.

> "If I understood only one thing,
> I would want to use it to follow the Tao.
> My only fear would be one of pride.
> The Tao goes in the level places,
> but people prefer to take the short cuts.
> If too much time is spent cleaning the house
> the land will become neglected and full of weeds,
> and the granaries will soon become empty
> because there is no one out working the fields.
> To wear fancy clothes and ornaments,
> to have your fill of food and drink
> and to waste all of your money buying possessions
> is called the crime of excess.
> Oh, how these things go against the way of the Tao!"

Lao Tzu. Tao Te Ching, 53

Although yang is more valued in climbing, as mentioned above, it is more than necessary to know how to use yin to be successful. A very basic example: think of anyone when they start climbing for the first time. Their focus is on their hands and their arms. They will think that if they are strong, they will be able to do it and if they fail it is because they lack physical strength and need to go hit the gym. However, the key to climbing is in the feet —which would be yin in this example—, in placing them correctly so that they provide sufficient support from which to move forward, in trusting the grip and stability they provide, in building a solid base from which to progress. To raise and place the feet to reach higher or better hand holds rather than raising the hands and pulling up on the feet, even if it is dragging them up the wall. Technique versus strength. Thinking versus acting.

Our muscles are stimulated during the day, but at night they replenish and grow while we sleep. When we try to climb a route and we are testing the steps, our brain will integrate them when we stop testing, without us doing anything, so that we can move forward when we try again.

The practical proposal that can be drawn from this would be to educate our perception to better understand, value and use the yin aspects, integrating them with yang, compensating —or avoiding— their excesses in a conscious way, maintaining the so precious and delicate balance. To open space for passivity, observation, integration and adaptation. To be subtle.

Subtlety

> "Look for it, and it can't be seen.
> Listen for it, and it can't be heard.
> Grasp for it, and it can't be caught.
> These three cannot be further described,
> so we treat them as The One.
> It's highest is not bright.
> It's depths are not dark.
> Unending, unnameable, it returns to nothingness.
> Formless forms, and image less images,
> subtle, beyond all understanding.
> Approach it and you will not see a beginning;
> follow it and there will be no end.
> When we grasp the Tao of the ancient ones,
> we can use it to direct our life today.
> To know the ancient origin of Tao:
> this is the beginning of wisdom."
>
> Lao Tzu. Tao Te Ching, 14

Subtlety governs our life and we must learn to see it and pay some attention to it. From yin (the subtle) comes yang (what manifests), so we should not underestimate its power or ignore it. As I mentioned in the previous chapter, our focus is on the yang, on what is seen, the superficial, the material, the external. However, many of the difficulties we may encounter are rooted in subtlety. Identifying what is subtle, what we overlook, can lead to great transformations.

A superficial problem (yang) has its roots in the deep (yin). Some examples of subtlety can be thoughts, beliefs or ideas. Our climbing is conditioned by our fear of falling, influencing the whole experience. When you reach the step you are afraid of, your body unconsciously lowers its hips and flexes its legs preparing to face the fall rather than to overcome the step. The excuses you make predispose you to fail. The internal precedes the external, a single thought sabotages the whole project. The mind (subtlety) overcomes the body. The small overcomes the big. A single word of encouragement can substantially help the achievement of a goal. The idea precedes the reality. Visualizing the steps before climbing, besides situating us, serves to convince us that we can do it. The subtle is like the code behind a video game or an app: it cannot be seen, but it determines what can and cannot be done. Not being used to thinking in these terms, our tendency is to face problems directly with force, from the dense. If we cannot send a project, we think that we lack strength, that we have to keep on trying and trying.

> "Water is the softest and most yielding substance.
> Yet nothing is better than water,
> for overcoming the hard and rigid,
> because nothing can compete with it.
> Everyone knows that the soft and yielding
> overcomes the rigid and hard,
> but few can put this knowledge into practice."
>
> Lao Tzu. Tao Te Ching, 78

However, we are not used to work with this subtle part. Maybe we are executing a step in the wrong way, maybe we don't trust our belayer enough, maybe we are not placing one foot correctly, or we may be afraid of falling because of a past experience. Many causes can be found in subtlety. So, applying force or trying harder and harder, even if it is a (long and painful) way to overcome an obstacle, is far from being the most efficient. What manifests outside (in the yang, in the dense) gives us the clues to know what is happening inside (in the subtlety, in the yin), giving us the opportunity to recognize hidden "codes" in us that we could manage or change. Looking deep inside us, at the roots, at our beliefs, at the small details, can make a much more noticeable difference with much less effort and suffering.

One small step in the wrong direction can lead you to lose the trail and have to make your way through the vegetation until you find your path again. It's not climbing the route over and over again until you reach the top that leads to success, it's finding the right combination, the right information of moves. When visualizing a route, if we fail to see the right step and we wrongly internalize it, then when we are tensely hanging off the wall it will be much harder to adjust. If I rely on the wrong grip, I may never get the sequence right. However, a subtle shift in a foot's position can change the whole situation, allowing me to reach other possibilities that previously seemed too far away or too uncomfortable.

> "Act by not acting;
> do by not doing.
> Enjoy the plain and simple.
> Find that greatness in the small.
> Take care of difficult problems
> while they are still easy;
> Do easy things before they become too hard.
> Difficult problems are best solved while they are easy.
> Great projects are best started while they are small.
> The Master never takes on more than she can handle,
> which means that she leaves nothing undone."
>
> Lao Tzu. Tao Te Ching, 63

Subtlety is usually the base where everything else settles. It supports our whole being. For example, if you have an erroneous belief about your capabilities, it will accompany you in all facets of your life until you manage to change it. If, as you climb, you manage to develop more confidence in yourself, this new belief will permeate the rest of your life and create different results. From the subtle (the attitude) you will create the dense (the results in your life). It is invisible, deep, imperceptible work, such is its very nature, but it is of vital importance. It cannot be ignored or repressed, although we tend to do so. We must roll up our sleeves and get down to work. If we do not work on it, sooner or later it will reappear and will continue to make us stumble over the same difficulties, always limiting ourselves in the same spots. If we start climbing by pulling on our arms without learning to use our feet, we will be able to do well in very basic grades. We may even be able to do a route of a higher grade, generating the illusion of progress. But sooner or later we will hit a wall and realize we have to pay attention to foot technique to make any real progress.

When a problem manifests in your life try to look for the possible subtle causes. This is the best way to combine the two forces. Observe and accept the yang to know, appreciate and care for the yin. Climbing shows us when conflicts arise that may be rooted in subtlety. For example, when we are afraid of something irrational, get frustrated at our limitations or make absurd excuses and justifications. In turn, you can allow yourself to experiment with small changes in the details and observe how a new situation opens up. The rigidity of always doing the same thing is contrary to life. Believing that we already know everything, that there is only one way to do things, even though we always end up failing in the same places. However, the soft and flexible find their way and reach everywhere, like water.

We must stop imposing and trying to control everything and open space for possibility. Many things are not the way we think they have to be and, perhaps, we should explore possibilities that had not crossed our minds before or that we had overlooked because they were so subtle.

Letting go of (excessive) control

The need for control is predominant in our society. There's very little space in our daily lives for flow and improvisation. We want to plan everything, make sure we don't miss anything, even though it is often impossible. Trying to manage everything is an impulse, a counterproductive need many of us have, although it may seem productive at first. I believe that control is a yang characteristic, and the ideal would be to keep it in balance, just like everything else in our lives.

Safety during climbing is something to keep under control. Correct use of protective gear, having the equipment in good condition or applying safety techniques correctly are some of the aspects that cannot be overlooked at any time. However, the safest thing to do would be to stay at home on the couch (even if it has its own risks, such as the loss of health in the long term caused by a sedentary lifestyle). It is in that balance between assumable risks and controlled risks that any activity takes place. If we want to make any progress, it is always necessary to surrender a little to uncertainty, to leave what we have under control and expose ourselves to change, to growth, to discovery.

When we want to grow and progress, we focus on doing, on effort, control, speed or effectiveness. However, the growth of anything is organic and slow, so it cannot be forced. It is like planting a tree: we just have to plant it and take care of its basic needs and it will grow. Always at its own pace, there is nothing we can do but wait. If we overwater it, it will rot. If we add too much fertilizer, it will get nutrient burn or, perhaps, yes, it will grow faster, but it will be very weak or its fruit won't have much taste. Haste makes waste, as we say.

> "The Tao never acts with force,
> yet there is nothing that it cannot do".
>
> Lao Tzu. Tao Te Ching, 37

Our growth works exactly the same way, in the balance between doing and not doing, training and resting, trying and reflecting. Not forcing but flowing, respecting the natural process. We have to let go of our expectations and accept the slowness of life, its organic and natural rhythm. It may not coincide with the pace we would like to have, but it is the way it is. We can't always be more, have more, or try harder. Sometimes we must be less. We must let go and see what happens. Let the universe —or the tao— manifest itself. Imagine yourself fighting a climbing project, a route you'd like to send that you're working toward. When you're stuck on a sequence, it's not always helpful to persist to exhaustion. It is much more effective to try it once or twice and rest. Or even leave it for a few days to reflect, integrate the movements, leave space for your mind and body to make new connections.

> "The living are soft and yielding;
> the dead are rigid and stiff.
> Living plants are flexible and tender;
> the dead are brittle and dry.
> Those who are stiff and rigid
> are the disciples of death.
> Those who are soft and yielding
> are the disciples of life."
>
> Lao Tzu. Tao Te Ching, 76

By pushing too hard, we are more likely to do worse and worse. As we get more and more tired, we will have less and less strength and it will seem more and more difficult. This will take its toll on our attitude. Trying to control too much and forcing situations will create an imbalance that will have to be compensated in some way, as we have seen above. An imbalance that will manifest itself in the form of, we could say, "side effects". Going back to the example of the project we are struggling with, the most obvious side effect of forcing too much could be an injury. But there may be more, some more subtle, such as not allowing room for growth. If we try the same thing over and over again because we think it should be done a certain way (we tend to think that we control how it should be done) we don't leave room to discover, to learn. To illustrate it with an example, it's like when we are holding a grip with our left hand and we find it impossible to reach the next one. If we stay in that position, without leaving room for the possibility of it being different, we may never move forward, because the moment we change our hand and take the grip with the other hand, the position of our whole body changes and this new perspective may make it easier for us to place our feet so that we can easily get to the next grip. And this is part of the process, this trial and error, changing and trying new things are a necessary part of following the natural order. To allow things to happen.

> "It is easier to carry an empty cup
> than one that is filled to the brim.
> The sharper the knife
> the easier it is to dull."
>
> Lao Tzu. Tao Te Ching, 9

This need for control is usually rooted in fear. Fear of what is different, of change, of uncertainty. It is the attachment to our expectations, to what we believe should be, to a certain outcome. But the tao teaches us the opposite: everything is change and everything is in a continuous dynamic balance, formed by the different imbalances that are generated and compensate each other. Thus, clinging to something goes against the changing natural order. It would be more advisable to let go of what is not useful and adapt. Do what is necessary at each moment, learn —or unlearn— what is necessary at each moment. You may have learned to climb by pulling on your arms, but that won't work if you want to keep progressing. As the difficulty of the walls you are climbing increases, you will have to learn new techniques and unlearn the tendency to do everything with the strength of your upper body. From the fear of falling when you were starting out you learned to lock your arms to stay close to the wall. When you evolve and start to feel comfortable climbing you must unlearn this mechanism and learn to rest in situations where there was tension before. You will have to empty yourself of what you thought was best in order to try other things that open up new possibilities. And so on constantly, without resisting too much. To try to make something go the way we want it to go is to deny all other possibilities. Let go of your labels, stop thinking about how things should be and make room for how they really are, surrendering to the infinite. Allow possibilities to manifest that you never even imagined and, in this way, you will be able to process and manage them properly. To do this, you must reconcile yourself with emptiness, with the void.

The Void

Emptiness is just as important as anything, any "something". It is simply another part of the tao, necessary and complementary to fullness, completeness. The void is another of the yin elements that we find a little difficult to manage. It makes us uncomfortable, even a little afraid. Nothingness, emptiness, silence. Having nothing to do at the weekend makes us more anxious than being busy, so we pack every last minute with activities, with the result that on Monday we are more tired than we were on Friday. Silence in a lift with a stranger makes us uncomfortable. If we have a second to spare, we take out our mobile phones and check the latest updates on social networks —I've even seen this happen at traffic lights while driving—. As soon as we feel a little hungry — empty stomach— we need to eat and we might even get cranky if we don't.

But emptiness is much more useful and powerful than we think. It is necessary to create everything within it. Sound arises from silence. Music is a combination of notes and silences. The white background allows you to read these words written in black. Our heartbeat is divided into systole and diastole, pumping/sending blood and relaxing/collecting, emptying and filling.

> "Thirty spokes are joined together in a wheel,
> but it is the center hole
> that allows the wheel to function.
> We mold clay into a pot,
> but it is the emptiness inside
> that makes the vessel useful.
> We fashion wood for a house,
> but it is the emptiness inside
> that makes it livable.
> We work with the substantial,
> but the emptiness is what we use."
>
> Lao Tzu. Tao Te Ching, 11

If you have time, you can enjoy more things and better than if you are continuously busy. A wall is climbable thanks to its cracks, hollows and imperfections that can be grasped, complementing the emptiness of the rock with our hand or our foot.

What makes the view from the top of the mountain so beautiful? Exactly, it's the emptiness again. Being high up means that there is nothing in front of us, so we can see everything.

It is from nothingness that all possibilities emerge. Facundo Cabral used to say in one of his songs: "Busy hand is a lost hand. The conqueror, by taking care of his conquest, becomes a slave of what he conquered". To keep climbing up you must be able to let go of one hand. How many times have you seen yourself in this situation? If you let go of one hand you will almost certainly fall, so you hold on until you get so tired that the only thing left to do is to release and let go of your efforts. We return to the balance I spoke about in previous chapters. If we were to look at climbing from the perspective of our hand, it would be a dance in which we grab something and let go so that we can grab something else. Open/close, full/empty, and so on.

But emptiness is especially relevant when it comes to our mind. The same that cannot stop still for a moment and needs to be stimulated and give its opinion at every moment. For thousands of years, various philosophies have been proclaiming the emptiness of the mind through meditation. Anyone who has managed to empty their mind for a few minutes will know its benefits. Climbing we have this possibility. Indeed, I would say it is a requirement rather than a possibility. How could you climb while thinking about other things? Finding the right foot position or feeling the slight shift of our body weight to one side is very difficult if we are thinking about what we will do next week, whether we have to take the car to the garage or whether someone is watching us or not. We can only move in the middle of a wall if we put aside whatever is going on in our minds and fully concentrate on what we are doing and what the immediate next step is. By freeing our mind of thoughts, we will achieve mindfulness, focus. Again, out of emptiness comes fullness. When you think you know how to do a move or what grip to take, all you do is constantly fail. If you keep repeating and repeating, the solution may come at some point, but it will be by mistake. However, if you empty yourself of your prejudices, of what you think you know and start to explore and discover new movements, new grips or foot holds, or new ways of positioning yourself, it is more than likely that you will find the solution sooner. Trying the same thing over and over again will always lead to the same results. You are repeating the same step several times and you can't execute it; you always fall. Tired and exhausted, you go home. The next time you go back to the same route, you instinctively start to do it differently and it comes out with incredible ease, you find the perfect combination as if without effort. When you emptied yourself of your efforts, the right sequence "appeared".

Unlearn to relearn. Empty yourself of thoughts and fill yourself with the rock, the present moment.

> "One who seeks knowledge learns something new every day.
> One who seeks the Tao unlearns something new every day.
> Less and less remains until you arrive at non-action.
> When you arrive at non-action,
> nothing will be left undone.
> Mastery of the world is achieved
> by letting things take their natural course.
> You cannot master the world by changing the natural way."
>
> Lao Tzu. Tao Te Ching, 48

There is a popular story about a young seeker of knowledge who goes to the old sage's hut to learn something new, but when he gets there, the seeker goes on and on about what he knows to show how wise he is too. The old sage patiently listens to him while he pours tea into a cup until it overflows and spills out onto the table. At the old man's impassivity, the young seeker is alarmed and points out the obvious fact that he was spilling the tea. To this the old man replies that his mind is as full as the cup, and that if he is unable to empty it, neither he nor anyone else could teach him anything.

Expectations, preconceptions, prejudices, desires, ideas, theories. All this does nothing but limit us. It limits our perception to what we are looking for, leaving no room for discovery, for the new. When we look for something specific, we don't find something different. When you climb a route looking for a higher grade, you may miss its beauty, its aesthetic movements, the feel of the rock or the views around it. If you think the route goes to the right, you will hardly see the holds on the left. At least until you fall, abandon your preconceptions and open yourself to the possibility that the path is not where you thought it was.

At other times you are tense looking for the next grip to make the move and you can't find it, that crimp where you can fit a couple of fingers doesn't appear and finally, exhausted, you fall. Then you relax and search calmly. You realize that the grip you needed was in front of you all along and you were looking for it higher up for some reason. Like when you look all over the house for your keys and they only appear as soon as you stop looking for them.

Another case could be when you are climbing a route that has a more or less average difficulty, with good holds and easy moves, and then suddenly you come across a difficult step. Probably that step is not so difficult, and it is probably not the most complicated you have ever done in your life, but as you were used to a type of rock or a simpler type of holds, this step seems quite difficult, simply in contrast to the rest of the route. Your mind had a prefabricated idea of what the whole route would be like, and when your expectations fail, it leaves you confused and uncertain.

Your success or failure will depend on the speed with which you empty yourself and rethink what you need to overcome the new situation. And this is how we connect with reality, the best way to live in the present moment. Accept the constant change that is the essence of the universe and change with it. To flow. Water that stagnates corrupts and rots. If something is not as you thought it would be or doesn't go the way you wanted it to, just flow, don't get stuck in your preconceived ideas. Because forcing something to be the way we want it to be is totally counterproductive as we may be swimming against the current. Sometimes it is necessary to fight against the current for a little while, but if we see that it is totally ineffective, it is better to let go before we drown from exhaustion. Maybe downstream there is a branch to hold on to.

Another Taoist tale that illustrates this concept very well: the tale of the old man and his horse.

An old farmer had a beautiful horse. His horse was admired by all his neighbors, and he constantly received good offers to sell it, offers that he always refused despite being extremely poor. One day his horse disappeared, it ran away.

His neighbors came to console him and to remind him how much he had lost by not selling it: "What bad luck! Now you have neither horse nor money. We are sorry."

To this the old man replied, "Bad luck? Maybe, maybe not. We'll see." The neighbors were puzzled and took him for a madman.

A few days later, the horse returned to the farm accompanied by a dozen wild horses. Then the neighbors came back: "You were right, what good luck!"

To which the old man replied, "Good luck? Maybe, maybe not. We'll see." Again, the neighbors were puzzled by the answer, wondering how it could not be good luck to go from having one horse to having thirteen.

Soon after, the old man's son, trying to tame one

of the horses, falls and breaks his legs. The neighbors return to visit him to judge the situation: "What a misfortune! Your only son, the one who helped you in the fields, is now bedridden."

To which the old man replied: "Misfortune? Maybe, maybe not. We'll see."

The neighbors understood less and less. How could his son's situation not be a misfortune?

The following week, a war breaks out against the neighboring country. The military comes to the village to recruit the young men for an almost certain death in the war. But the son, having broken legs, is not drafted. The neighbors, tireless, visit the old man again: "You are so lucky, old man! Our young men are going to war and your son will soon recover and be spared the fatal fate."

You can imagine what the old man answers: "Maybe, maybe not. We'll see."

Emptiness is uncertainty. When we know for sure what is going to happen our experience is full of the expected outcome. And it is also good in its own right. When I want to cook pasta, I simply wait for the water to boil. When it reaches one hundred degrees, then I can cook it. Everything goes smoothly, just as I expect it to. However, we live in a world in which uncertainty is more prevalent than certainty, changes are many and faster each time, demanding high levels of adaptation.

Recent events such as the pandemic or technological

disruption test our ability to deal with uncertainty, with the void. With the present, letting go of the past. We tend to think that the unknown, the new and uncertainty brings loss, risk, scarcity, threat. However, it also contains joy, gain, happiness, abundance as it is part of duality, of the natural yin and yang balance that we have been talking about for a while.

Just because you're hanging on to a good grip now doesn't mean you won't find more as you go along. Besides, if you stay there for too long you will eventually use up your energy little by little and you won't be able to move forward.

On the other hand, in certainty and the known there can be joy and happiness, but there are also doses of pain and suffering. I believe that the saying "better the devil you know than the devil you don't" is a great fallacy that invites us to suffer just because we want to keep what we have at any given moment, contrary to what the changing nature of everything might recommend. Just because we are used to one thing, it does not necessarily have to be the best. Therefore, the only way to preserve peace of mind is to accept and embrace whatever comes, to use it as it comes. Remain open and receptive to discovering new possibilities, new experiences. Adjust the sails following the changing winds and simply sail.

Wu Wei

Wu Wei is the application —or the "non-application"— of everything we have been seeing throughout the previous chapters. The way of flowing with the forces we observe and with the balance of the universe. The term is often translated as "non-action" or "effortlessness", although it goes far beyond these simple definitions that remind us more of a praise of laziness and passivity than a way of living in accordance with the nature of things. Wu Wei does not really mean doing nothing, but rather doing without forcing, without disturbing the natural harmony and balance of things.

It is a kind of intuitive intelligence that allows us to recognize how and when to act in order to be efficient with respect to the nature of things, without applying counterproductive energies or energies that oppose a certain reality. Recognizing patterns, tendencies or principles that govern the nature of any given thing in order to achieve what we set out to do using the least amount of energy. It is as simple as not going out to climb when it is raining. You simply know that you have to wait for the rain to pass and for the rock to dry and that it would be stupid and dangerous to go when it is wet and slippery. It is that flow with the conditions that determines this model of efficient action. How we manage our resources so that we can get the best out of them. Doing when we must do, resting when we must rest. Applying the necessary action —no more, no less— to each situation. I climb slowly and with precision when the wall demands it, and fast and with strength when I am on the most athletic steps. I rest if I reach a ledge or if I can wedge my body into a crack. I identify the best way to grab a grip or to place my foot, the one that allows me to hold myself with the least possible effort and at the same time allows me to reach the next steps. The strongest person does not climb better, but the one who knows how to best use his strength. The one who knows where to place his feet, and when. The one who knows where to hold on, and how and when to make a dynamic movement and when to make a more static one.

To be like water, which always seeks the path of least resistance among the rocks of a river or through a mountain. Water flows, without imposing itself more than necessary, discovering its course more than making it. This is the philosophy that climbing has adopted throughout its evolution. Since it began with primitive materials, hammering the walls and filling them with pitons, ladders, fixed ropes, and other equipment that sought to reach the top however possible, climbing has evolved to aim to climb with the minimum amount of material and influencing the mountain as little as possible, in a more technical way, as Doug Robinson has already precisely defined:

> "Technology is imposed on the land, but technique means conforming to the landscape. They work in opposite ways, one forcing a passage while the other discovers it. The goal of developing technique is to conform to the most improbable landscape by means of the greatest degree of skill and boldness supported by the least equipment..."[3]
>
> Doug Robinson

But it is not all about doing something or not doing something —which is also a way of doing—. It's also about trusting and letting yourself go with the situation, without resisting. You may be hanging from a grip and tend to block to keep your body and your center of gravity close to the wall. The more you block, the harder it will be to hold on and the more energy you will be expending, until you can't anymore. Later, however, you discover that simply dropping your body to where it naturally falls results in a better grip, your feet gain grip, and you can visualize the next step much better and execute it with much more energy. This is the difference between positioning the body and letting it position itself. Gravity is not our enemy; it is our dance partner. We use the force of gravity to climb. By leaving your weight on your feet you get the necessary grip. By

---
[3] A Night on the Ground, a Day in the Open. Doug Robinson.

placing your body under your arm when you grab a small crimp, you make what seemed difficult even comfortable, using only your weight and this natural force. That's what climbing is all about, knowing how to balance the use of gravity with our impulses against it, to bring us upwards. Throwing your hand into the jug and resting comfortably inside it while supporting almost the whole body. Two opposite but complementary forces. We have already seen it, yin and yang. Well, the same here.

Knowing how to recognize the forces requires skill and concentration. No one said that "not doing" was easy. The most suitable metaphor I can think of would be climbing on sight. Without having experienced the route before and without any prior information other than what can be observed and felt, the climber begins to climb, must see the best moves for each situation and the best way to execute them. On the fly. An experienced climber is skilled enough to make this identification intuitively, without effort. They recognize the patterns of the rock and the possibilities it offers. They know how to use their strengths to take advantage of every opportunity provided by the rock shape at every moment, naturally, without overthinking, flowing through the route, light, focused and effortless —or at least no more than strictly necessary—. Accepting objectively what is there: the holes for your hands or the cracks for your feet, the closeness or remoteness of the bolts, or whether it is a shorter or longer step. Without thinking about how you think it should be. Without judgment. This is Wu Wei, the acceptance of the Tao, of the way things are in themselves, not how we think they are or how we would like them to be. Acceptance to be in harmony with oneself and reality. Feeling, observing, contemplating. If there is something that is not going the way you expected, do not force it because you can break it.

If there is a step that does not come out in a route, you can try again several times, repeat from the beginning or look for new ways to tackle it, but always without forcing to avoid injury, knowing when it is best to stop, when it is best to empty yourself to be able to return with the clarity of those who are not forcing themselves and have also let their body and mind integrate the new situation and the new movements. As we said earlier, it is about accepting slowness and that a plant grows at its own pace, not at the pace we want it to. We already know that life is a continuous balance between doing and not doing, between yin and yang. We must seek to maintain that balance and flow with it instead of producing more imbalance that later would have to be compensated. Even climbing is always in balance; no matter how yang the climbing, the effort, the will to grow and climb higher, we always have to come down. We will always come back to the point of balance. The higher we climb, the more we need to come down. The more we train, the more we need to rest. The more we force, the less we get. When someone starts climbing and begins to taste the satisfaction it produces, they may also start to climb too much, obsessively, forcing. The problem with this is that sometimes it is not an organic process. We go from not climbing at all to climbing every day and thinking about it all day long. The person may endure that imbalance, but most likely that initial pull is followed by a big stop caused by injury or simple boredom or exhaustion. "Bite off more than you can chew" is often said in the popular proverb to refer to this imbalance.

Another element that works against Wu Wei is an excessive focus on results. As mentioned in the previous chapter on the Void, expectations and preconceived ideas can be factors that hinder our fluidity, our ability to identify the flow we should follow. If our goal is to sail into a certain port and we have the wind somewhat against us, we can always adjust the sails so that we use it for our purpose. It will undoubtedly be slower than if we had more favorable winds, but we must accept the conditions and do the best we can with what we have, without being attached to the results we expected. It may take us a couple of days longer to reach port, but that's the way it is. Or maybe the next day the winds will change, and we'll get there even sooner than we set out to do. If, instead of accepting and flowing with the situation, I decide to take a shorter but more dangerous route in an effort to act, to control the situation, I may end up shipwrecked and not reach any port at all.

Another way in which Wu Wei could be interpreted would be "not interfering". Try not to manipulate or influence the natural course of things, just seek the path of least resistance and flow with it.

In psychotherapy, Viktor Frankl coined the terms "Hyper intention" and "Paradoxical intention" which, in my opinion, can shed some light on understanding the functioning of the Wu Wei.

Hyper intention happens when we maintain an excessive intention in what we want to achieve, so that the realization of what is desired is prevented. For example, if what you want is not to fall or to send a route, thinking excessively about it will cause just the opposite: that you fall or that you don't manage to send the route. Maybe it's the pressure or lack of concentration, but the more afraid you are that something will happen, the more likely it is that it will happen. How hard the last meters before the anchor are!

It's like when you have an important event the next day and you find it hard to sleep. The more you want to sleep the harder it will be.

Well, to counteract the effects of hyperintention, Frankl proposes a somewhat peculiar tool: paradoxical intention. Instead of wishing for something not to happen (such as falling), paradoxical intention would consist of just the opposite: wishing for what is feared (falling) to happen.

It is about stopping the tendency of trying to evade or control outcomes. One even tries to deliberately make what is feared appear, desiring it and exaggerating it if necessary.

Going back to the example of falling while climbing, the paradoxical intention would be to wish to fall. You would say to yourself: now I'm going to climb this route and I'm going to fall as much as I can. That way I will learn to fall and see that it is not a big deal. What do you think will happen? You will probably fall much less, you will climb with more self-confidence and, if you fall, you will have achieved your goal!

In the case of insomnia, the paradoxical intention

would be to set the goal of not sleeping to combat the hyper intention of wanting to fall asleep. The task now would be to avoid falling asleep, having a greater sense of control over whether you achieve it or not. In this way, I will most likely fall asleep as soon as I divert my attention to something else. Alan Watts called it law of reverse effort or the backward law:

> "When you try to stay on the surface of the water, you sink; but when you try to sink, you float."[4]
>
> Alan Watts

"Not Doing" works a bit like this too: when we try to control or do something seeking a result we may be interfering with some natural process, creating an imbalance or opposing some force (forcing a situation).

In the book The Way of Chuang Tzu, there is a story that can illustrate this situation of effort. Chuang Tzu —or Zhuangzi— was another of the oldest and most important Taoists known. The tale goes like this:

> "When an archer is shooting for nothing He has all his skill. If he shoots for a brass buckle He is already nervous. If he shoots for a prize of gold. He goes blind or sees two targets He is out of his mind! His skill has not changed. But the prize Divides him. He cares. He thinks more of winning Than of shooting and the need to win Drains him of power."[5]

[4] The Wisdom of Insecurity, Alan Watts
[5] Translation by Thomas Merton

The need for control or the search for specific results inhibit our ability to flow, to adapt to situations, to perform according to the needs of the present moment. There are times to act and times to let go. Many things improve without our constant intervention, which far from helping to solve something, tends to complicate things even more. It's like dropping your keys in a puddle. If you stir the water and it gets cloudy, you can't do anything to make it clear other than wait for the sediment to settle to the bottom and allow you to see clearly. The more you do, the more reaction you cause and the more reaction, the more you want to do. In the end it all ends up muddy for nothing. But when you let it be, the sediment settles to the bottom and the water clears up on its own, you observe where the keys are and deftly dip your hand to pick them up precisely, avoiding muddying the water again.

Knowing this you will be able to be calm and confident even in the most complicated or rushed situations, responding naturally and spontaneously, with skill and efficiency, emptying yourself in every moment to accept reality as it is and not forcing how you would like it to be. Living in tune with life, instead of fighting against it.

Harmony

Everything is perfect just the way it is, there are no mistakes in the design. Everything is part of this unity that is in constant change and in permanent balance at the same time. When you accept these basic principles, you will begin to identify this harmony present in the world.

You can choose in which parameters to interpret the universe. You may be conditioned in all sorts of ways by previous experiences or by your close environment, but you will always be in time to dismantle these schemes and create new ones that better adapt to reality. Stop judging based on wrong standards or obsolete paradigms. Integrate a new way of perceiving the universe.

> "The Tao of the universe
> does not compete, yet wins;
> does not speak, yet responds;
> does not command, yet is obeyed;
> and does act, but is good at directing.
> The nets of Heaven are wide,
> but nothing escapes its grasp."
>
> Lao Tzu. Tao Te Ching, 73

In the West, when we see the yin and yang symbol, we commonly understand it in a simple way as "everything good has something bad in it and everything bad has something good in it", but the reality is that nothing is bad or good, we simply judge it that way depending on where we put our focus. Just as using force would be "good" at certain times and "bad" at others, perhaps at different times we would be better off climbing more technically, resting, observing or looking for a more stable position.

The reality is that all parts form a process with each other. One part is constantly being born from the other, moving forward, growing together and feeding back. Our way of recognizing these parts and observing their interaction is by contrast. You must be hungry to enjoy food. To know what we want, we must also know what we don't want. If you don't like someone, it's because you compare them to someone you like. If you like something, it's because you don't like something else. We have to see one side to recognize the other. And this way of comparing is what gives us the measure of the world. This is why we have to be careful and be aware of comparisons, because they condition our criteria too much. Comparing ourselves with other people is and has always been an eternal source of dissatisfaction. You know your climbing level because you compare yourself with others through the grades you are able to climb. The moment you compare yourself with something or someone a few things happen. First, and going back to the example of the grades, you are not taking into account many of the variables. The grade, the difficulty you are able to overcome, is only one variable in the satisfaction you can get from climbing. Enjoying the day, the company, climbing in flow with nature around you and amazing views... it all adds up, but it can't always be lumped in with the grade you're climbing. Comparing yourself to a grade or difficulty (or someone else climbing it) will make you focus too much on that aspect alone, causing you to feel a sense of inadequacy if you don't make it, as well as missing out on other parts of the experience. From your perception of what you want comes what you lack. Let's take another example, if you compare yourself to other people who have more money than you, you will be focusing on what you lack, and you won't appreciate what you do have. If we keep talking about money and richness, you are probably already rich compared to a good part of the world. But maybe you should not compare yourself with anyone directly because, although it seems to you that others have more money than you, they might just be someone who lives in appearances and does not even enjoy it. Or maybe it's someone who chases money so much that they don't have the time or the ability to enjoy nature —which is mostly free, for now at least— or to go climbing, for that matter. Beauty emerges from ugliness, abundance from scarcity, what we judge good from what's bad... and the other way around. And so on, as we pointed out in passage number two of the Tao Te King, quoted in the chapter on balance.

But be calm. It may be necessary to compete, compare or chase grades to stay motivated for a while or to begin to better appreciate the rest of the experience. It's all part of the journey and there is no need to try to be perfect (because everything is already perfect).

Everything has its place and is perfectly necessary, if only to complement their counterpart. What may seem to be in opposition or in conflict, is actually cooperating with each other, generating and self-regulating within the Tao.

When you begin to recognize the harmony between the different external elements you can put the focus on the most interesting part of all: the harmony between your inner and outer self. The way to navigate through life without unnecessary tensions, without swimming against the current, without fighting useless battles. But be careful, this does not mean to not fight, it is rather to look for the intelligent way to do it. Identify what can work in your favor and use it, instead of battling with what is more difficult for you. David didn't take down Goliath in hand-to-hand combat. He threw a stone at him from a distance, using his intelligence and aim. Ghandi, although he did not throw a single stone against the army and police, who were much stronger (brute/physical force) than he and the rest of the people who joined his revolution, did manage to liberate India.

The way to achieve this harmony is to know —and accept— oneself. But to really know yourself, just as you are, without expectations or filters and without judging, just observing yourself. Knowing your possibilities and your limits, just as you are. Do not force yourself trying to fit in where you cannot. Adapt to your reality. If you are trying to climb a difficult route and right now you can't, you keep falling and getting frustrated, don't force yourself. But I'm not saying quit or don't try hard. Just focus more on your strengths, your possibilities. Instead of struggling and wasting your energy, find the smart way to achieve what you have set out to do. Maybe you can train more or better, develop a better technique, think of a new sequence, rest, observe, use a different grip than the one you are using... You can stop for a bit and try again later; the rock will still be there when you get back. We've all seen someone who is unable to recognize their weaknesses and thinks they can do it all. And we've also seen this type of person fail miserably. The one who thinks he can climb anything he wants just because he is strong. More than one route ends up putting him in his place.

Don't get attached to the wrong things; to wrong approaches. And, again, do not judge. What looks like a weakness can become a strength, just as a strength can become a weakness. A hole in the wall may seem difficult for us to grasp because of its shape and we judge it as a bad grip for our purpose. However, as we climb the wall, we realize that it works perfectly if we hold it as an undercling. The gap was not "bad" in itself, rather the approach was wrong. You were using it the wrong way. It was a "good" grip in its own right, in its own category as an undercling.

Another story by Chuang Tzu illustrates these concepts in a very interesting way: The Useless Tree.

> "Hui Tzu said to Chuang: I have a big tree, The kind they call a "stinktree." The trunk is so distorted, so full of knots, No one can get a straight plank out of it. The branches are so crooked you cannot cut them up in any way that makes sense. There it stands beside the road. No carpenter will even look at it. Such is your teaching. Big and useless. Chuang Tzu replied: Have you ever watched the wildcat crouching, watching his prey. This way it leaps, and that way, high and low, and at last lands in the trap. But have you seen the yak? Great as a thundercloud he stands in his might. Big? Sure, He can't catch mice! So for your big tree. No use? Then plant it in the wasteland in emptiness. Walk idly around, rest under its shadow; no axe or bill prepares its end. No one will ever cut it down. Useless? You should worry!"[6]

There is a place, use and function for everything, even if we don't know how to see it at the beginning. Everything that happens to us, everything we do and what we do not do, every event in the world.

---
[6] Translation by Thomas Merton

A big mistake can become a learning experience and a future success, an illness can teach you to take care of yourself and to enjoy life more.

Reality may not always fit your plans, but reality may have bigger plans than you could ever plan for. Also, as limited beings, we don't always create the best plans because we lack information. So, having your erroneous expectations not met is almost a favor you could be grateful for. We are very biased, and we pursue things we don't want, don't need or don't fit into. We focus on one part and are unable to see its counterpart. Just as in the previous story, Hui Tzu was only focusing on how useful the tree could be to produce wood. However, the tree had other possibilities. Moreover, thanks to this "uselessness" it will be able to live many years in peace. In its "weakness" lies its strength. No famous climber could have pushed the limits of the humanly climbable if they had been a good engineer or a good doctor. At the same time, they could not have made a name for themselves without a good doctor to help them recover from their injuries. Everything has its place, and it is not the same for everyone, even if it is hard for us to see it and many people aspire to be a straight tree for someone to make desks out of them.

Alex Honnold, the famous climber starring in the movie *Free Solo*, seems like a shy, introverted person with a "little obsession" with climbing walls. However, with the growing popularity of climbing, someone came up with the idea of making a movie and Alex shot to worldwide fame in and out of the climbing world. For someone who is happy living in a van, eating simple food straight from the pot and climbing walls, this fame can bring nothing but imbalance. The imbalance that comes from having to do videos, interviews, commercials... and whatever your audience and sponsors ask you to do instead of just climbing. When you just want to climb for the sake of climbing, climbing for money is something that comes at a cost. To make a living off climbing you need enough time and money to support yourself and travel, but, from there, it's all superficial. But Alex finds his way to correct this imbalance: not to feel forced by his fame and possibilities to do something simply to make more money, he has turned that strength into something greater. He does it to have a positive impact on the world. Through his foundation, he funds various projects that promote access to solar energy around the world. This way he finds motivation to deal with his obligations as a climbing star without feeling like he's selling out too much. Avoiding the feeling of doing things he doesn't want to do for money he doesn't need.

Most of the time we do things because we think we have to. We believe we have to pursue certain goals that are not really the most suitable, the ones that will bring us the most happiness, well-being or satisfaction, so we waste our one and only life trying to fit in where we cannot and trying to please others to see if we fit in, ignoring our own nature, leaving aside our own place, where we could develop our being according to our own standards. Thus, the teacher ends up being a lawyer, the artist becomes a dentist and a large percentage of young people want to be civil servants to live in that illusion of security, certainty or comfort. Success or failure depends on who judges it. For some, success will be having money, being famous or having power. For others it will be having time, wisdom, love, satisfaction, or climbing walls every day or only on Sundays. We cannot and should not all fit the same standards. Each person or thing can find their own way to live satisfactorily, according to their own circumstance or nature. The Ugly Duckling thought he was ugly until he discovered he was a swan. A seemingly useless piece of rock can become the engine of a town's economy thanks to climbing's rise in popularity. Again, a tale from Chuang Tzu: The Turtle.

> "Chuang Tzu with his bamboo pole was fishing in Pu river. The Prince of Chu sent two vice-chancellors with a formal document: "We hereby appoint you Prime Minister." Chuang Tzu held his bamboo pole. Still watching Pu river, He said: "I am told there is a sacred tortoise, offered and canonized three thousand years ago, venerated by the prince, wrapped in silk, in a precious shrine on an altar in the Temple. "What do you think: Is it better to give up one's life and leave a sacred shell as an object of cult in a cloud of incense three thousand years, or better to live as a plain turtle dragging its tail in the mud?" "For the turtle," said the Vice-Chancellor, "Better to live and drag its tail in the mud!" "Go home!" said Chuang Tzu. "Leave me here to drag my tail in the mud!"[7]

To summarize: to be in harmony with the universe and with oneself it is essential to accept all things — especially oneself— as they are, without judging them or using them wrongly. Remember that everything is perfect, there is no useless situation or skill, and everything depends on how you approach it.

Steve Jobs mentioned the concept of "connecting the dots"[8] in his famous speech at Stanford University.

---
[7] Translation by Thomas Merton
[8] https://www.youtube.com/watch?v=UF8uR6Z6KLc

In it he says that dropping out of college was the best decision of his life, although he was very scared when he did it. But, when he did, he stopped going to the classes he attended out of obligation and started attending the ones that really interested him, even if they didn't seem useful to his "career" at the time.

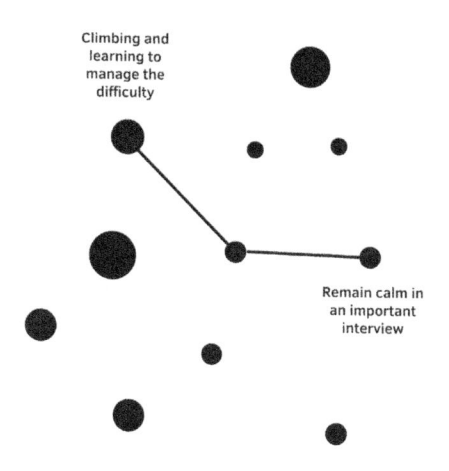

Climbing and learning to manage the difficulty

Remain calm in an important interview

One of those useless classes he attended was calligraphy. Ten years later, designing the Macintosh, he remembered what he had learned in those classes. The Mac was the first computer to include different typefaces and fonts. And so, the "dots were connected". It's impossible to connect them by looking into the future; you can only see the connection when you look back.

Anything can be the raw material for something good. Just trust the course of nature, everything will find its usefulness in one way or another. Just relax and flow.

Flow

We could say that climbing is like the Tao. Something that can be felt, intuited but not intellectualized. Balance in movement in which so many variables intervene that it is almost impossible to rationalize. You might be thinking or following someone's advice on how to tackle a movement or where to shift the weight of your body, how to place your feet or where to grab a crack. But you won't get anywhere unless you integrate it as part of you, unless it flows through your body.

That's climbing. Flowing over the wall, without the need to constantly think about how to position yourself or where to move from. You don't have to think about it because you already know it. And if you don't know it, you will have to learn it, to go through the process of merging with the route, of finding the right combination to get it.

Physical strength is something necessary, but it plays a rather secondary role. Climbing is more about knowing what to do with what you have. With what you find on the wall. It's in you, not in your muscles. There are many cases of professional climbers who get injured and stop training for a long time and, even when they come back on the wall with their atrophied muscles, they are able to resume from a very high level without too much effort.

To flow is not always to let go. It is rather adapting to the circumstances, finding the best way to do something with the situation you encounter. Always skillfully, with precision. Maximum effectiveness with minimum force: we are talking about technique, efficiency.

When you try a project over and over again, what you are really doing is looking for a way to align yourself with the route, to merge with it, with its nature, with the forces that prevail in it. You may need more physical strength at some point, but it will not always be a prerequisite. On many occasions you can choose which forces you want to use. Different forces could be a better use of your feet, a better distribution of your body weight, identifying better grips or gripping them in a different way, among many other variables. Recall a route you now perform effortlessly and think about how much it took you to master it in the beginning, while you were immersed in this process of aligning yourself with it, of finding the combinations.

A single crack in the wall can have thousands of possibilities: it can be used as a right- or left-hand hold, an undercling or side pull hold, or as a foothold when the hands are already looking for something higher up. All these combinations are like the notches of a key that open the lock. If they are not the correct ones, the lock will not turn. And if we force it, we run the risk of breaking the key and damaging the lock. The key must fit the lock and not the other way around. It's the same for your climbing. You cannot change the rock or gravity, it is you who must change, who must adapt and work with what is there, not with what you think is there or what should be there. Empty yourself of the wrong prejudices and do not try to impose yourself on the wall or gravity —they are much stronger than we are— but skillfully use everything you find to achieve what you set out to do. We must correctly use all the imperfections of the wall to support your body thanks to gravity.

That is the difference between influencing and flowing. We think we can influence how things are; sometimes we have our hypotheses about how they should be, and we try to impose ourselves. On the contrary, to flow is to accept, to adapt to what is there using our resources, but without trying to impose ourselves, without forcing three fingers into a two-finger pocket hold.

And we do not force ourselves in this process either. We respect ourselves and take our time to do things because we know the cyclical nature of all things and we respect the natural order. We live the whole experience, with its ups and downs, in resting and in pushing, in moments of action and in moments of reflection, in yang and also in yin. We know when to move our hands, when to move our feet or when not to move. We are in the here and now with all that it entails. We neither avoid nor deny any of the parts. We use what we have. We do not seek or desire anything different. We are happy and at peace with what we are doing in the moment, without focusing on the future or the results. Without running back and forth chasing goals and objectives that upon reaching them become bigger and farther away, keeping us in dissatisfaction.

When someone starts lead climbing, fear causes their focus to always be on the next clip, where they are going to place the next carabiner. Their mind is so focused on that those distances seem insurmountable, the distance between the clips seems more dangerous than it is, and their body tenses up, resulting in poor energy management and a greater chance of falling. The harder they try to reach and clip, the farther away it seems to be. The more they chase the security of being clipped, the more their own insecurity becomes evident, and the more it affects them. And when they reach the bolt, the anguish does not end; they discover that the next one is even farther away and that they have much less energy.

However, more experienced climbers, while being aware of the risks to which they expose themselves, they simply climb. Without paying too much attention to chasing the clips, they climb the route as a whole, discovering the best combinations, resting whenever they can and need to, and pushing when the situation calls for it. They enjoy the whole process without paying too much attention to the result.

They know how to choose where to put their attention, even when a wall seems smooth to other people's eyes. When everything seems difficult or even impossible, the climber finds the holds, discovers the way by focusing on what is there, identifying the possibilities, the part that suits them at that moment.

> "To understand the small is called clarity.
> Knowing how to yield is called strength.
> To use your inner light for understanding
> regardless of the danger
> is called depending on the Constant"
>
> Lao Tzu. Tao Te Ching, 52

You must mobilize the necessary resources, at the right time and in the right way. And, moreover, spontaneously. I'm sure you've experienced this on some route. This is what is called "being in the zone". The moment where everything flows, everything fits, you find the grips and your hands fit them well, you support your feet and they feel firm, your mind is relaxed, free of fear or any intrusive thoughts. The Wu Wei level of perfection, effortless action, integrated action. Because there may be thousands of teachers or trainers or coaches or whatever, but to learn to flow you must do it by yourself.

Only you can know how much force you must

apply to a given grip to hold yourself, without over-tightening and wasting energy. Only you feel where to shift the weight of your body to accompany you in a movement. Only you can differentiate which is the perfect crack to place your hand in, even if it is not the biggest, the closest, or the one you would like. You must find this kind of connection yourself. You can't pick it up from a book, there is no method, there are no shortcuts. It comes with patience, through practice, observation and awareness. Getting to know yourself and your universe more and more. Real knowledge —practical wisdom—, like the one you get by climbing and you don't know how to explain. Not like the intellectual one, which accumulates information and, in many cases, without knowing how to interpret it —until the time comes to put it to use and we realize that we didn't really know anything—.

Anyone can reach these levels, through climbing or any other aspect of your life, you just must be receptive to reality and let it flow through you, without forcing the path, but just walking it. Discovering it at every step. Embracing and using whatever presents itself as a complete experience, from the most yin to the most yang. Managing the balances and imbalances. Observing, flowing. Step by step, following the natural rhythm. Climbing and living.

> "The tallest tree
> begins as a tiny sprout.
> The tallest building
> starts with one shovel of dirt.
> A journey of a thousand miles
> starts with a single foot step."
>
> Lao Tzu. Tao Te Ching, 64

Glossary

Belayer

The person who stands below the climbing line and, through the appropriate belay device, handles the climber's rope. He uses his weight to counteract the effects of a climber's fall, thus ensuring the safety of his partner's ascent.

Bolts

Usually referred to a plate and a bolt that are the metal elements fixedly anchored to the wall along sport climbing routes. Placed every few meters, they allow the climber to place his quickdraws and place the rope through them, preventing a fall beyond the last bolt through which the rope has passed.

Chuang Tzu

Also known as Zhuangzi or Chuang Tze, was a philosopher of ancient China who is estimated to have lived around the fourth century B.C. He is considered the second most prominent taoist, behind only Lao Tzu and heir to the latter's thought. The book that bears his name (in some translations it is known as "The Way of Chuang Tzu") gathers an amalgam of writings that transmit taoist teachings through stories, anecdotes and short dialogues.

Climbing grades

An element of information consisting of assigning values that grade the difficulty of a route. They serve mainly to help us decide if a climb is within our possibilities or not. The most commonly used grade scales in sport climbing are the American and the French scale, but there are many more.

Climbing project

Select a challenging route with the goal of sending it.

Climbing sector

Sectors are areas within a climbing area or crag, composed of a set of routes.

Climbing shoes

Special shoes used for climbing, lightweight and with grippy soles.

Clipping, to clip

Refers to the act of placing the rope through the carabiner of the quickdraw, which will be hanging on a fixed bolt.

Free climbing

Climbing using only one's own skills, without the

aid of materials to progress in the ascent. The only equipment used is for protection in case of a fall (such as rope, harness, belays and fixed anchors on the wall).

Lao Tzu

Also called Lao Tze, Lao Zi or Laozi is a Chinese personality whose historical existence is debated. He is considered one of the most relevant philosophers of Chinese civilization. It is estimated that he lived between the sixth century B.C. and the fourth century B.C. He is credited with having written the Dào Dé Jing (or Tao Te Ching), the essential work on Taoism.

Lead climbing

Climbing the route passing the rope through the bolts as you ascend. A route is considered sent when it is lead climbed without falling or resting on the anchors.

Quickdraw

Two carabiners joined by a sewn sling that are used to attach the rope to the fixed anchors of the route, hooking one carabiner to the plates of the route and passing the climber's rope through the other.

Route

A climbing route is the path a climber uses to climb a wall. Sport climbing routes are usually equipped with fixed anchors that allow the safety rope to be placed along the ascent. They can have different shapes and characteristics and are graded based on their difficulty.

Sending, to send

Climbing a route (leading) from start to top without falling or using artificial anchors to rest or progress. The anchors and other protection material are only used as a safety measure, but not to facilitate progression.

Sport climbing

Climbing modality understood more as a sport practice that consists of climbing walls of different difficulties equipped with fixed anchors placed to protect the climber's safety.

Tao

Tao can be translated as 'the way', or also as 'the method' or 'the doctrine'. In Taoism it refers to the primordial essence or fundamental aspect of the universe; it is the natural order of existence, which in reality cannot be named, in contrast to the countless 'nameable' things in which it manifests itself. In different translations Tao can be referred to as the way of heaven, nature or Dao among others.

Tao Te Ching

Also known as Tao Te King or Dao De Jing, it is believed to have been written by Lao Tzu around VI B.C. and is one of the fundamental texts of philosophical taoism, as well as influencing various currents of thought throughout its long history. Its title can be translated as 'The Book of the Way and Virtue' or 'The Book of the Way and Power'.

Taoism

It would constitute the set of teachings dedicated to the Tao. The present book is based on philosophical taoism, on the tao as a system of thought based on the original teachings collected mainly by Lao Tzu and the book of the Tao Te Ching. It is important to differentiate this concept of philosophical taoism from the concept of religious taoism, which is composed of different belief systems that mix elements of philosophical taoism, Confucianism, Buddhism and local beliefs of China and Southeast Asia.

Top rope climbing

Climbing with the rope already mounted on a top anchor so that the rope is always above the climber. It is the safest way, ideal for beginners.

Wu Wei

It is a term of chinese origin that describes an important aspect of taoist philosophy, according to which the most appropriate way to face a situation is "not to act", rather understood as "not to force", using in a harmonic and efficient way the resources that each situation provides.

Yin Yang

These are two basic concepts of taoism, which are used to refer to the duality that this philosophy attributes to everything in the universe. It describes the two fundamental opposing and complementary forces, which are found in all things, complementing each other, generating each other and maintaining the balance between them. Yin is the feminine principle, the earth, darkness, passivity and absorption. Yang is the masculine principle, the sky, light, activity and penetration.

Taoist Readings

Tao Te Ching, Lao Tzu
Recommended translations:
— Ursula K. Le Guin
— Richard Willhelm
— J.H. Mcdonald

Chuang Tzu
— *The way of Chuang Tzu,* translation by Thomas Merton

Tao: The Watercourse Way, by Alan Watts

Subscribe to keep finding wisdom on the rock with us!

climbingletters.com/mail

Printed in Great Britain
by Amazon